Free Verse Editions
Edited by Jon Thompson

the atmosphere is not a perfume it is odorless

Matthew Cooperman

Parlor Press
Anderson, South Carolina
www.parlorpress.com

Parlor Press LLC, Anderson, South Carolina 29621

© 2024 by Parlor Press
All rights reserved.
Printed in the United States of America.
SAN: 254-8879

Library of Congress Cataloging-in-Publication Data on File

978-1-64317-460-0 (paperback)
978-1-64317-461-7 (pdf)

1 2 3 4 5

Cover design by David Blakesley.
Cover photograph and closing photograph by Matthew Cooperman.

Parlor Press LLC is an independent publisher of scholarly and trade titles in print and multimedia formats. This book is available in paperback and ebook formats from Parlor Press on the web at https://parlorpress.com or through online and brick-and-mortar bookstores. For submission information or to find out about Parlor Press publications, write to Parlor Press, 3015 Brackenberry Drive, Anderson, South Carolina 29621, or email editor@parlorpress.com.

Contents

Of Poses	4
Precarity	5

•

Snow Globe	8
No Ode	9
Postlude	14
Precarity	15

•

General Syntax	18
Gun Ode	19
Major Lure	22
Song	23
Wall Ode	24

•

Difference Essay	27

•

Appears / Disappears	39
Hive's Lament	40
Precarity	41
Standing Figures	42

•

the atmosphere is not a perfume it is odorlesss	45
Mother Ode	50
Precarity	53
Laughing Man	54

•

Respiration Ode	58
My Wife's New Desk	60
Repair	62

•

Late Music	72
Country Mulligan	73
A Field Mentality	76
The Weight	77
Bouquet	78

•

Notes	85
Acknowledgments	87
About the Author	89
Free Verse Editions	91

I harbor for good or bad, I permit speak at every hazard

—Walt Whitman

There is a right side of history and it is love

—angel Kyodo williams

I would meet you anywhere western sun meets the air

—Jay Farrar

Of Poses

    viral migrations bedevil our sleep
    we rise to raise a body flag   flown
        our town among the rushes   how it
    rushes darkness   the wheeling of stars
    in the chittering dust   an aerial smallness
        scales our very hubris   surface   skin
    touches our wings   binds us awake
           enmeshed to what we cannot see

        surfactin   the two-brained logic of the lungs
        gyres in fever and kindness   principles
    go recognized and ignored   our demos breathing
        gets sticky   on all scales   things   wakes   up
        for we can cast a form like a dandelion bloom
    to heed a material blindness of the senses, yes?
        —the commonest of poses

Precarity

...*the sad marvels*, what
sad marvels

to C & B's for coffee
being born   Tuesday
morning   off to work

not off to work

a lifetime watching
the clock   the lawn

the passersby weary
unmasked or dog

the neighbor's child grown
the actuarial imagination

•

To see and be seen
on the street

exposure and protest
being on your feet

street wise or country proud
the line   and what does not
cross it

crossing it

O

Snow Globe

It was January 6, I was six years old, which would've made it
        the 60s, and it was snowing.
Snow filling trash cans like ashtrays. Ma and Pa
    distantly fighting the giant snowstorm.
I jellied the donut in my fist and dragged my Cheeto fingers
        over the walls of the igloo.
Quiet murmur of voices muted by the snowy insulation.
                Snowy machinery.
      A blue sky blower somewhere else dreaming of sun.
Here it's snowing and my snow castle is growing cold.
Cold like white poodles falling from the sky.
Cold like Conrad Aiken killing his children.
I am watching *Silent Snow, Secret Snow* all alone, Orson Welles
        booming about snow, the igloo growing close,
            an undone cave. Rosebud—

Snow that seems miles away growing close on a sled.
        Snow like the subject of Being battling the poem.
      Squid vs. Whale, Firebird vs. Camaro, Turgenev vs. the Wolves,
Ahab, etc, all heavenly white machinery made in a snowy world,
        it was the 60s, and it was snowing.

No Ode

I.

The infinite caste and the soluble membrane, the papers
    of a wasp. "Earth has nothing I desire besides you…"
Not a hand nor a bird nor a bicycle, never the one for delay…

Systole: remembering the days of his youth it was *ba-boom*, not
    happening. As in square, *ba-boom*, the box.
Not the sense of style but the sense of impending monument.

A cruising altitude of 30,000 feet is not anywhere close to heaven.
Never sky: "a place where nothing, nothing ever happens…"

On a Wednesday at the Capitol something did happen, not the dream
again deferred, not the righteous bear nor the know nothing snake
    just the sickening spell of blood. In this way wound, green

not happening. Bad harvest, knots of locust, a western pyring
    of all scrub lands. "So as to speech the lily goeth, so as
        to seed the gentle deer goeth…"

In the bare trees after the late storm there was one thing (a dead
    cardinal) against some things (larch pines) against
everything (a snow tableau). Call it what you will: a man at a window.

Threshold: in my head the great debate of worth and self-loathing.
    In the Mayan calendar a constellation of zeroes in the 21st century.
        Zot, king of rendering, and Self, queen of disease.

Yet in Gerald Stern a benign fibrosity, and an attachment to old felt,
    and a memory of coal dust,
            and the color of blue lentils,
    some metonyms against the void.

Not motive or asseveration. Not a result of living as experiment
    but living together. Every lab a vial filled. Not a sea

full of oil, nor an office full of bluster. Not a corporation,
        nor the October morning moving
    to incorporate a neighborhood.

Astor Place, not status. A marble salute
        and an incoming bomb, who is wearing
            an impervious hat?

Come toward me now, my no generation, the image of less

    from space

            as we're moving

  away

|

So goes mercury into the fish, so plummet the man from the cliff.
    If it were nothing there would be no landing, no attempt
at distillation at the funeral, no calving glacier, no trial,
        no flooding, no letting, no shining beam at Ground Zero.

    Noh, as in theatre, everyone caked in astonishment.
"No!" as in the bad date, the shadow too close to the body.

Everywhere in the marshes a thousand resting cranes. Legs up, a *P*

        signing *here, here, here,*
how the impulse to deceive is a fear of profusion,
    my soluble membrane, your rage,
        what's missing in a poem.

II

White fog lifting & falling on mountain brow
   Trees moving in rivers of wind
     The clouds arise
as on a wave, gigantic eddy lifting mist
  above teeming ferns exquisitely swayed
        along a green crag
   glimpsed thru mullioned glass in valley rain

All the valley quivers, on extended motion, wind
      undulating on mossy hills
  a giant wash that sank white fog delicately down red runnels
    on the mountainside
   whose leaf-branch tendrils moved asway
    in granitic undertow down—

No imperfection in the budded mountain,
   Valleys breathe, heaven and earth move together,
     grass shimmers green
sheep speckle the mountainside, revolving their jaws with empty eyes

The great secret is no secret
   my skull and Lord Hereford's Knob equal,
    All Albion one

sings Allen Ginsberg to William F. Buckley, an August night, 1969, and I am six in the television glow, and I am alive in the rising wind of Albion, something strange on my father's brow, something strange in the shining teeth of Bill Buckley who is one, and I am one, and my father is one too. Savage deceit in the smell of war. Pop rustles the sheaves of the **CHRONICLE** and calls Buckley a major prick, and smoke curls upward from the ashtray, and all of moody heaven's starless black.

III.

Who begets whom in the grammatological afterlife?

Here, the spell of occupation. Here, the joy of willow green,
      willow green after rain, call
and response, response and call, someone

is on a lamp post, someone's "Holy, Holy, Holy…"
    goes the lamb rudely stolen again. See it on the counter
        of nyet! All languages for all things, not

              the mind simply perceiving
        the instance, brachial droplets of blood
evenly spaced, prostration of bodies
              in street puddles and bright signs.

    Not a tanker on earth at sea
        full of cheap cargo, nor the sea like a gray hill.
          Not me, not mine, not-in-my-name.
      Not you in my orchestration
        of you, not simply the
              rote roll of days.

    Not Buckley with his Bircher gun
    Nor Ginsberg in his windowpane
    Not Albion nor his father, nor his Old Father Weary Blues
    Not Naomi in her psych ward, nor my mother in her chair
    Not my daughter in a psych ward, nor the students in a line

In my country "men, their rights and nothing more,
      women, their rights, and nothing more," the Land
    its rights and nothing more in my country

This is a history poem   This is not true   In my country there is
    no history but the lesson we didn't learn

Now the seers of my ears awake

        Now the whys of my eyes open

                In my country of soluble membranes, the papers
of a wasp aflame, my country

is no Albion, and my country desires the rack,
        the crumbling façade and the pothole, the poison
          in my school

I am here at the park and I am here in the court and I am here

           in the bed of my country, no has a voice, and a system
        on parole, no will not stop in my country

Postlude

Aftermath, if we can
call it that, the meaning
of the blues

persons' loves of life
discerning the subject
and the subject

Patriotism, Patria, etc—
I like to worry male desire,
how it is pointed unpleasantly
at you, a shocked person
with a country

Heroes return as comics, apologists,
TikTok, the sound of rain
on a VA hospital window—little
solace heard from Curiosity on Mars

Still, I owe you something
and worry the silence between us
the more you are silent

Change, that is, a stutter
ing national terror, I think
there'll be room for singing
but it's just exhaustion

Nerves end near their victim
My anomie, like a public troll,
revolts the sky and holds up
a shattered window

I, Thou, We—cannot add the manifest

Admit the paean is over
and there'll be a person
to show—you, with your
untrained voice still howling

Precarity

To see and be seen
by others

not the voice
but the face

voice in the face
mouthward

the warbler
now
in the coffee tree
broken and free

•

In hunger   by migration
to see the living
and be seen
to have taken it in

the scene and all
its decline

the moving picture
in sepia hues

the map made body
blushing blue

blood   a precipitate folly
in wheat or oil

rainfall's mean
in the morning dew

General Syntax

A better world shall emerge on account of this. A general is just
as anybody, events, places, things I could tell you to make
a nerve end squeal.

Age wrinkles the body, withers the tome. I want so much to become
meaningful, meaning to be understood, the events, places, things
which relay force. Always there has been some loss on some shore.

Americans never quit, 24/7 openness, we will be prepared to say
something, do things. I am an old soldier and so see war from
far away. I mean this literally, as I am on Venus watching the unusual
gas activity on earth. Always there are interests about.

Build me a son, I say, and I will show you a river. There, in my
dreams I hear footsteps, crying, the green rustle of reeds. In war
there is no victor if you consider the reeds. The sedges, by contrast,
were always on the up and up unless we slept there.

It is fatal to enter the sedges, and it is part of life. Life is a lively
process to fail winningly. I mean victory, you win some and you
wake up with a deep feeling, as far as anybody is concerned.

As far as anyone is concerned life is a lively process, as is empathy.
Syntax you'll have to do yourself, like an old soldier marching
everyone into the tomb. Age wrinkles the body.

Our government has kept us within borders, as do governments
do by law. Part of the American Dream is in the borders, where they
hover. The best of luck is to be born into some kind of dream.

The soldier, above all others, is an American who never quits.
The soldier, above all others, waves his bayonet. The world is in
a quandary over unusual gas activity. Interests lie. O build me
a son toward openness. There is no security on earth.

Gun Ode

A dollar with a gun in its mouth, a daisy with the sun
in its mouth. Dream is a noun for possibilities, as in
everything reminds me of threat

Learning to live in opposition, accretion, the catalogue of parts
to their parts—where have all the flowers gone?

        Gun—what have you done to our bodies?

A ripping, then a keening sound, fresh chalk marks in the square
    If what you've got is a country sickness, seek cause
as the cure, push the paper pace, register, register,
dismantle the 'gun figure'

        My hands don't fit the bitter hasp

As in, naked and afraid, without means of protection, we were
forced to love and evolve

As in, O America, aren't you tired of being an ode, why don't you
ever use your Kevlar® shield?

    O First Responder, thank you also for being America

Once in high school, going to a gun range somewhere in the live oak
hills, maybe it was a quarry, it was foggy, Scott Olson had an Uzi, and
he sprayed out a bloom of bullets that surprised us all, it was foggy,
remains of the red squirrel glowing everywhere

    If what you remember haunts you change the ghost

If what you've got is a problem wrapped in prayer, dismantle
the problem's conflation, unwrap the ammo from the prayer

        Gun—breathe back your noxious vapor, unstain
the trigger finger, clear the site, the tower, the stage, friend up a glory
in something other than a flag

This is not a memory, I am not at war, you are not a shooter,
and I am not afraid, my shoulder's stuck on the wheel everyday

But them Russians, them Russians, and them militias, too, not your
huddled masses shot in their Sunday pews

Unbolt Unbolt Unbolt Unbolt

If what you've got is a cache spend it in flowers

Recall Recall Recall Recall Recall

Whose hands need harms, what threat these times?
A queer shoulder and a disabled wheel, melanin stupidly
    caught in the wheel

America, you're the safest country in the world from intrusion—
    Pearl Harbor??   9/11??
Compare that with, well, just about anywhere…
    Why do we need a gun?
Exactly who are we fighting if the enemy is within?

    Beretta   Bersa   Smith & Wesson

        Browning   Colt   Mossberg   Glock

Ban   Ban   Ban   Ban   Ban

I shot a blue jay once with a pellet gun, it sickened me for an
hour watching it die in the rotty creek behind my house

If a vision of earth, all of ours, if the color of dust and pollen,
everyone's dust and pollen. All or nothing or nothing at all,
will the American dog ode eat its foot?

Ban   Ban   Ban   Ban   Ban

I am writing this poem in the pall of fresh sulfur, another school,
another disgruntled white male—to say it—a cut cut cut like a rat-a-
tat-tat, the vermin high in the sky or behind the wheel

If a more general male viciousness, then something to dispel

That That That That That

What can we grow in a garden with too many holes?

      Remington   Ruger   Savage   Steyr

         Winchester   Uzi   Sig Sauer

Drop your weapons!   Disarm your alarms!

A kid at camp—Friendly Pines—lost an eye one summer
in the mountains of Arizona, a .22, I think his name was Derrick

Mitch, an old friend, he drifted, dropped out—I heard he
got shot robbing a liquor store near Fresno

My wife's best friend fought demons, lost, he blew his head off with
a shotgun for Thanksgiving, his name was John

I can't think of one happy memory ever associated with a gun

    Disarm   Disarm   Disarm   Disarm

If the impulse to destruction is greater than the insight to love
    we are doomed to a garden of graves

If freedom is money spent on guns, what is American grace?

        Gun—your time is waning

In the stupid west wind you are rising against yourself

I am not a shooter, I am not afraid, I gather my army of flowers

    a dollar with a dream in its mouth

        a daisy with the sun in its mouth

Major Lure

Could I have but one moment to remember, shine and fear,
where were we, what bright shore? It's duty, honor, country
in that order of concretization, they told us that.

I am concerned for the general's well-being as I do not think
our stratagem is well understood. I mean I have just returned
from events that lead me to believe bullets wrinkle the body.

I suppose in a way I have known every war, though that old
scoundrel rarely played by country. The rules being the biblical
injunction against sleeping with another century. There are
bound to be insidious marches, sedges.

My first recollection is that the foot knows more than it can say,
and we should've listened to that, the morning fierce in birds
we thought were wires. Bang.

Never give an order you intend not to keep. Young soldiers
always die, and the tragedy is for what order of belief? Duty,
honor, country, color, region, grudge, town, biome, blood.
These are areas of concern.

One cannot wage war with old soldiers. Under no circumstances
should their sleeping be disturbed. Our country is now fit
for an ailing king. There is no substitute for the facts,

which are they died hard, those savages. Our enemies are about us
as we are about them, in the world, I mean, self-hatred, no escape.
Objects relay force and place. Years wrinkle the skin while

our enemies wither in chains. On an island, you are remembered
for a duty cleaning cells. March came and went with nary a breeze.
This country I am concerned for, as is anybody for their home.

Song

through burdens
and addictions
and solitude
and shame
self-deception   vain
glorious
and rue

                    this is what
                    carries us
                    the weight
                    of love

Wall Ode

More such living mass come in than any single other try
The mass, I mean the people, where they come
And go a possible portal, chemical, reaction always
In their shoes, a quantity of cells, a process cleared
By HQ, and the gate—an arch—a kind entrance
Definitionally, an invitation, American experiments
In eye says I, what resides inside a door, why
The border is a breeder and a gateway not
A wall, the wall is hollowed empire lines
To unclimb, unladder, more a newfound
Trellis bloom than any single other try, mass
I mean the quantity, selves as cells, a you applied,
A many in the one, delivered skin enough for time,
Equal measure vessels come to brave us to the end

Difference Essay

This is a story about difference. I never knew about difference, like what is a difference story? There's nothing different under the sun, all things, all things are different.

I began with a simple thought, What is difference?[1], and how and who, each one of us a provisional throw, contours only, intimations, as if there was something else besides shapes, to make shapes, I made this different.

> A thought is a separate world connected to a body, this illusion for many years, is it different from yours? Different from the usual mind/body, which is, by definition —
> something strange from mine.

Reading the script, each becomes whole in the will of the fourth dimension.[2] Mine becomes clear in the frame of my autistic daughter, how very different from yours. The barbarities of immediate experience dictate flight or restraint or laughter. When she sees a path she chooses it, hill and dale and stranger's door, how we are lost in the woods.

> But there is no community in this difference. Despite spontaneous meetings, "hello stranger!," this is a lonely planet. I am trying to get off of this planet, a difference ideology with thrusters and footnotes that might be but tragically isn't so very different from anything else.

---

[1] http://www.amazon.com/s/?ie=UTF8&keywords=different&tag=mh0b 20&index=aps&hvadid=1696582112&ref=pd_sl_4a9qij3rnt_b: or whatisdifference.com
[2] pure will, or Gurdjieff, the Fourth Way

Rocket, or genome, if mine is like yours in the exact calibration of 'this not that' then there is no essential difference to anything we ever do. Ever, aver, assay, say, "a pain in the neck" to try and measure what is different in a person.[3] People are different from water, are different than air. My person is different from yours and takes offense.

> Surfacing is this crisis in brambles and parking lots, a daughter representative of the day relentlessly spent. Sometimes a kind of belief, "rest awhile, stay, lean...STOP!" We are born locally and we run away locally no matter what the theory says.

>> Thus, my ambition, my ambition to individuate, to find a ledge to rest, a care or cure for the sameness of this hard life. Some lock of hydra against chemistry or a mutating chromosome. Saying things, "I began with a thought..."

>> So it is, and so it goes on, green and gray, the cognitive woods, our uniforms getting smudgy, getting blurry from repetition in all this selfhood, personhood, lost in the woods, mad and tragic people with hoods.[4]

---

[3] See Andrew Solomon, *Far From the Tree;* or Bukowski, "The Genius of the Crowd": "there is enough genius in their hatred to kill you/not understanding solitude/they will attempt to destroy anything/that differs from their own."

[4] White hoods, black hoodie, hoods are different

Green not blue, and four not three, ah, yes, little family of difference. And so a lock against the self who would make a family the same 2.2 of our readily recognizable wakefulness.

> She has a G tube, a green tube not blue tube, a plastic port from world to gullet, a mission straw, a food bloom. She does not speak, she does not chew, she does not blanch nor wonder. However pure or inconsolable, this mark on the body, her body, is a singular regard for one and so others.[5] For what they lack I lack, and I shall not assume...

In the smallest gear of cell there is something missing. The red wire not the blue from which you would say to anyone, "hey there! you on the edge of the sinkhole, stop, turn!"

But there is no turn, she does not turn. There is no turning back from this essential difference. I am color blind and you do not hear high C. These are marks in her protein bindery. O, mark upon her body—

---

[5] Levinas, *Totality and Infinity*, "The Other precisely *reveals* himself in his alterity not in a shock negating the I, but as the primordial phenomenon of gentleness."

When I left the hospital I had a sense of not being whole. Mine. And others. Sudden ailments of contour seen, something uncorked, unmet in the billowing hospital gown. Looking at these hands, these feet, I realize I am not some other—who is she? From the whole a hole, a fall, a gradual process everyday, through what has been familiar a world grown strange, gown strange, ever, aver...

>An extended past and an expected future. Between me and the other world there is ever an unasked question: unasked by some b/c of delicacy; by others through the difficulty of rightly framing it, "How does it feel to be a problem?"[6] So he says, wearing this self-same sheet of strangeness. Does she wear this self-same sheet of strangeness?

My daughter arrives and is unintentional. This is no illusion, the sort of being that keens and creates history. Able and awake I set off addressing the 'problem,' my solve bound up but spilling through the town, awake aware of some lengthy process which has occurred.[7]

What has occurred is occurring, again and again, and my cells drawn right into thrusters that hum empathically. Thus, to begin is to start anew. Thus, Tuesday, clean slate. To set out is to take a first step. To run or run after. Mapping the lurid interlude of language is one way to say "I am a missing person."

>Someone saw the person in the hallway.
>Someone saw my little girl down the street.
>O, that these problems were different...

---

[6] W. E. B. DuBois, *The Souls of Blackfolk*: Is this my double-consciousness?, I'm on thin ice, I'm lost in the woods.

[7] Charles Darwin, *The Origin of Species*: "A man preserves and breeds from an individual with some slight deviation of structure, and the improved individuals slowly spread in the immediate neighborhood. Species of all kinds are only well-marked and permanent varieties."

I began my story by noting the difference between X and Y, apices of why. Why could these things on a brilliant May day not happen differently? Who said you could choose your poison?[8]

    Point of view is exhaustion looking up.
    Point of view is the ocean coming through the trees.

        On my planet a slice of life is a slice of DNA,
        one view per slide at a party you have inevitably
        joined. I would join my protein to hers if it
        would be different. I would bind forever strange
        into my sleep.

But then I'd come to write of a terrible relentless
  sameness. The monochrome in the chromosome, the color
    of some and not others. Who is not other in the infinite
      catalogue of difference?[9] To be riven is a state. "The shades
    of the prison-house close round about us all."[10] Not to be
      multicultural is to miss that these are all cultures, agars in
        the jar, some frayed flavor we are drinking. How could I
          miss that these things were not seen and tasted by others?

---

[8] http://addictionsameness.blogspot.com
[9] Timothy Morton, *The Ecological Thought*, "What is a person? Nothing is self-identical. Organisms are palimpsests of additions, deletions, rewritings. We're embodied yet without essence."
[10] DuBois

In this way the self-consciousness that I yearn for you is not my daughter. My daughter individuates by not seeing this part of her obvious difference.[11] Yet where am I? A thought, a vanity, to share in this grief a new life. Alone, awake, the impostor and cruelty of ability. How dare I speak for her. Or what dark torment speaks?

> We are all so very close, and no man weaves his island to the sea. Rafts a difference, coughs and sleeps poorly. The one unknown, the one next to. "You there!," waiting to see and be seen. So very human, this membrane, the weave of a visible democracy, cell by cell, each one a different story, O Brothers, O Sisters—

Of the days of affliction there shall be no end. This is the weather condition. It is others' deficit to feel sorry for my daughter's lack. And yet our gladsome throng is not so very happy.[12] We struggle in the weight of privacy, building a difficult circle round our crew. Even as our strangeness solders us together, it's mood and misapprehension to others, and to ourselves. Identity or fate, joy, or explosive car ride, what we choose each day.

In this cruel fact my difference does not matter. But then it did, It does
Seeing the real deal of difference is how we are awake. Adaptive fish
full of plastics. The lone cricket creaking on the lawn, the obvious
nose on one's face, or the face of the rock, or the face of your
back turned toward me. I could not see difference, hear
difference and now I see difference, American cultural
weirdness in the woods of a brand-new century.
How to change this feeling into air? I would set the
scene by settling the score. Fuck you with your barred door.

---

[11] Lacan "The Imaginary order the mirror stage is a phenomenon to which I assign a twofold value. In the first place, it has historical value as it marks a decisive turning-point in the mental development of the child. In the second place, it typifies an essential libidinal relationship with the body-image" "Some Reflections of the Ego."

[12] Tolstoy, *Anna Karenina*: "Happy families are all alike; every unhappy family is unhappy in its own way."

What is a better word for plot, or where are we going? This try is
no different from any attempt I've ever made, maddening self-pity,
self-loathing. This is an essay—focus—get your head out of your ass!

    What would make this different? That letters could inoculate
blindness.[13] That skin is a conduit contract with a language sea
that is missing. A person is not a metaphor, our nucleic soup is
real. I choke on its gray brine.[14]

    Am getting nowhere, elsewhere. Years
really do pass, on a drive, in late spring,
"zippety do da," day after day, that we
could get out, move forward from the
moldering house. If the world breaks in its
misery is that company? How do I sign for
world pain?[15]

Whine of cracked window, November for interval, stripped trees in
the wind of a western prairie. Today I am very alone.
    This is my brutal democracy. I carry her verge into
    darkness or Wyoming.

---

[13] Cognitive inoculation? Access to sign? I research the deaf to learn to see
[14] Claudia Rankine, *Citizen*, "To live through the days sometimes you moan like deer.
Sometimes you sigh. The world says Stop that. Another sigh. Another stop that."
[15] neo-realism, post-fact, der Lebensweldt auf Trumplandia

> Birth, a free thought, the democracy of a baby, many
> babies, everyone someone's baby, pure possibility, space
> around the body, the air around, around sea[16], around a
> you or a me. It's the smell and the skin, the boundary.

Yet the unspecified future cannot rouse an empathy of cause.
You do not know what you authorize. How to see this could be very
different?[17] As it happens, the limit of myself is especially stark,
meaning proliferating, meaning a mountain of diapers. I neither
hate the stork nor hate my impulse to watch it leave the lake.

Chance or heredity, speech or stem?
      What kind of dog for her, and how about a pony?
         This   is   break   ing   down   the eyes of my daughter
    your daughter   we assemble together and form a bond
        in our attraction / repulsion is a society, and we
will get answers...

      That we loved you sufficiently, and took you to sunlight,
             that your face turned...

To share a privacy? To find a key to what is private in property? "It is not
from the benevolence of the butcher, the brewer, or the baker that we expect
our dinner, but from their regard of their own self-interest."[18] Adam Smith
knows, blue, not green, yours not mine in the limit of self-regard. In the
goulash of "all of the above" we are unhappy together.

---

[16] Brenda Iijima, *Around Sea*, "where physiognomy intuits intensity"
[17] Aliens, rescue us! That black lives matter, that saying so points out some don't, hominid or anthropod, my god or yours, if we can't get along intra-species, how in the world will we get along with different species?
[18] *The Wealth of Nations*

> And so it is we progress. I believed I
> progressed in a story, a story about
> difference. To stroke her head in the
> swelter of our pink walls...to digest a
> vacancy as activism or will...I cook for her
> and clean, a specific particle, modestly
> round ambition to shout and to jump.
> O hubris of the shining mind, what can I
> write to change?

Thus, I moved and became lonely to myself. I moved again and became rich with others. Our various bodies glowering against the world.

> Turning time into space, a wife a son, a silent daughter,
> glowing as the world. We make our days and will our nights,
> a 4D dream for limited mobility, our rocket awake and alive
> in this world of difference, things of difference. Pure laughter
> in this clammy land, a face blooming up from sleep.

Love: the vertical integration occurs at the horizontal section. We ride this insight like the flawlessness of will. The quickening mind is the believing mind, and that is a blue one, a red one. We see this in the model of the code. I, being we, for a stretch in time, a well-defined path with blurry boundaries, the code allows, is able, and so something different found us for a while.

        Something is broken in the reckoning of like and as. More this and this and this as day's insistence. More loom, as in far above, what towers the exceeding strand. A likeness or wantness to bind all that is broken. Not mend but gather, differently hand. The horizontal friend is right next to you crossing the street. What a funny gait!, and look how the rain falls on us all together!

I began my story, and I will continue my thought, and what you shall
    assume I will grant you unconditionally, or beat you senseless
        for assuming. Thus our futures in the sacred wood,
            the hand I write into difference neither shocked nor
                unafraid, the silence of my daughter / your daughter
                    signaling sound and sense in another
                  dimension. Empathy is being
              this happenstance rocket. It is
          not symbolic, this thing.

Appears / Disappears

Different World, what enables us
to live and be a better race?

The ordinary shoves up against the monumental,
there a summer darkness enlapses the city

A red fox appears / disappears
in the sulfurous glow, a woman
cleans up a piece of cake

Our job is to be both epic and tiny
between us the partially obscured

Later, a sun over Maryland
and we neither mesmerized nor bored

Postcards, memories of crowds nor especially
frightened, the little man sweeping the sidewalk

A local version of asymmetrical warfare
These things take time, we must attend and work

We cannot avoid global tensions,
the harms of the various climes

We have many common causes
here on earth, poverty and privilege
both an inheritance of childhood

Water and the need for cake
We riot together and clean the streets

Good will on both sides, no sides
Our target was home and others

Now we are monsters trumped
of all concern, not
everyone is a monster

Hive's Lament

Words cut down the tubs of our mortal keening.
Play the note slowly for the letters to rest.
Two or more players could last a lifetime.
What dialogue gives / takes away mere happiness.
To attempt the quiet bride loose the bridle.
Days go by and nothingness in signs.
How the bees hum going gatherings into sleep.
Each takes and talks remember into his arms.
Her arms green rushes of infinite swims.
Theys colors going a ghostlier demarcation.
Just like that the keening becomes a sign.
Comprehension incorporates endless bodies.
Slave to the thirst that makes grass grow.
Want for the bees to comb their honey hair.

Precarity

To see and be seen
by a specialist

someone trained
in the optic nerve

seeing the truest
part of you

a soulsay
or the haptic man

to pick up a racket
a scope   an urn

•

Reciprocities—
to see and be seen

not the mirror
but the error

not the vessel
but the vector

handed along the finch wings
the hedges of morning

not the echo
but the equal
a you   capillarial

bringing the stitching home

the hum and rum

Standing Figures

> *"I've never been able to understand the artist
> whose image never changes,"*
> —Lee Krasner

We see around things when we're seeing well
      The doves where the springs of the bay are
   The back of your neck on the sea

A life filled with taking it in—climbing, swimming,
    fighting, climbing,
              Rückenfigur—

glued to the horizon, blind cells jungling
    the creep of green,
        think of thirst, the sun of oblivion

Our eyes and minds as we look repaint the picture,
    but what if we'd rather not?

We see around things when we're threatened

Harmony's a lust, edge to edge, pooling
   our limitless resources, the palm of your heart
            on the sea

So many times by the sea, and not to see—

Ere our paths unseen will trodden have
   this spherey figure

To register agreement point to the foreground,
    ours, a changed body

    Collective solitaire never to let go
Eyes and minds paint figures before the sun

   We see round things when we listen

the atmosphere is not a perfume it is odorless

but we smell it anyway, methane, CH4, the ambient nose of combustible
fuels, driving from the airport (not old Stapleton, charmed now to brand
spanking condos) coming home to Colorado in the Aftertime,

and the bland tan buildup of roadside derricks I notice, and the haybales
surrounding them like haybales, Monet-style almost, except they're a wall,
a distraction, scrim, not grass at all but viewshed blocked,

disagreeable landscape pastoralized, disambiguation, whatever that keeps
meaning, painful as a sort of non-self, non-object-being-object,
not grass being eaten by an ass or cow, a material betrayal I feel

in the pumping of your dark heart, productive and shining in the late
afternoon plume, a bluegreen effluence titrated by a curated thirst.
Holy lowly recognition, Carbon O we've been had! Still

I'm low on gas and must hope, a substance held in the image of a balloon
memory, *The Red Balloon* floating in a clear French sky. Innocence, being
lost or being found out, my sense of time goes in and out of phase with

what must be yours, I know I feel it, dispersed and sometimes not
dispersed, as if I am gas also speaking to you, which of course I am,
the punchline of poetry. Are we always going to go over how I or you

do or do not smell the haloing over the Front Range? Home on the burner
boiling up the ether. We might jam the aliens (who is they?), the score
sheet's out, the action's evanescent, coal is a black or brownish-black

sedimentary rock formed as strata called coal seams, plant matter, time,
peat, heat, pressure over millions of years, former wetlands become coal
forests, progress, easy, to steam, way after Pennsylvanian

and Permian climes, in other words slippery. I didn't notice the smell last
time we drove from DIA (seen once, an endless tall grass prairie, again,
a series of sails, or a caravan of Conestoga wagons, another

inspiration of repackaged empire hugging the eastern horizon
like dancing auto-lot dolls. Sale! or Sail! Do I have to say it? material
dis discovery turned into lost baggage, no need to conflate

the smell of eggs into another thumb of odes, hyperobjects are
your organs, which, by and by, thrill me, churning at the mantle,
making need and want the same daily anxiety, will there be enough?

Scarcity is a woman on a bicycle in a gorilla suit throwing an egg.
Who isn't the target? I just feel you too heavily dispersed (just now
a Safeway baggie caught in the Russian thistle) which becomes

the lung of growth itself we share passing north, the new town
of Reunion (Come on Home!), welcoming us to a lessness not possible
as nostalgia but there nonetheless gaining traction in my scan of

red barn siding, TuffSheds®, play structures, plastic white horse fencing
the crisis in or out, and little false lakes growing up the rolling hillsides
of the South Platte river drainage that stretches lazily all the way

to the Missouri, passing Sterling, CO (Queen of the Plains,
né Arapahoe, Cheyenne, Pawnee, Sioux, Blackfoot, Kiowa, Crow, etc)
after it gathers its North Platte branch (now we're in Nebraska)

in the aptly titled town of North Platte, which was exactly a year ago
last drove, I mean in real time, our shared calendar of days the increment
we share, now bracketed, a different cene. Would that we had

a compound eye, wood we? And Lo! I have to stop, *running on empty*,
the dinosaur beckons, I tap my plastic fob and into the vessel
goes darkness, thirst, a series of hoses and wires made of you (with

the addition of ethyl alcohol to abet guilt and false consciousness),
the Niobrara Shales, sexy, fr the Denver-Julesberg Basin, a large
asymmetric syncline of Paleozoic, Mesozoic and Cenozoic sedimentary

rock trending north to south I remember (they're endless) another
stretch of I-80, a cosmic intuition night driving past the Sinclair
refinery (now we're in Wyo), and the plumes at night like towers

of gold on a burning galleon headed nowhere. Or the top of the Pitkin
parking garage (after Frederick Walker, two term CO governor who
smote the Utes at Milk Creek, and smashed the miners in Leadville

mining not silver, coal or even lead but molybdenum, alloying metal
crucial to American industrial might in WWII) in my Reunion,
standing with my stimming daughter (train obsessed) watching

boxcar after boxcar of Powder River coal going by (we counted to
100) as the sun glowed west against the hills, your glowering flanks
meticulously piled in open cars (open-top hoppers) and a point of light

like insight flashing at the break between, each time, the light of our
time. Now we're listening to Queen to calm the confused child,
("Love of My Life") *don't hurt me*, from *Night at the Opera* (the best,

don't give me no *News of the World* clap clapping the plexiglass at the hockey
game, see?), she's sad, we're sad, we're all so sad. But that disc I have
on vinyl, double-sleeved, I bought it new at Tower Records in SF,

just another excursion abetted by gas, its admixture blended seamlessly
with rock opera, how we went and returned on a fast jet plane?
I really have that question mark in my body because of you.

So so the golden years, or the Glorious Befores, I call them my carbons:
skis, urethane skateboard wheels, my father's discreet convertible obsession,
Fiat 124 Spider (blood red), '67 Ford Mustang (Steve McQueen blue),

a '53 Ford Sunliner, flathead V-8, first of the hotrods (lemon custard),
and saddest of all the (canary yellow MG) with the chrome not plastic
bumpers, which are oil, which I totaled on a drive

to the beach in La Honda a stone's throw from Alice's Restaurant.
The kids are alright, the kids aren't. Ken Kesey in my woods
making hot worry this way come. I remember

throwing gas on a fire at Big Sur, big time!, don't ocean me in, or a Bic
lighter tossed into the flames years later, its jet message burning idol
joining god & the lysergic acid in my head, or a hologram,

being six (someone told me, "you are six") at hips, looking out the rear
windows of the car (a '70 Volvo wagon) and the enduring fog outside
of Salinas ("Steinbeck country," my mom said) following an ancient

International Harvester dropping green fists of Brussel sprouts and
without warning, to the side of the road, a message from the reptile god,
a small mountain of tires on fire, burning black and orange

over the ghosty fields. Cars cars, and boats too, the agents of our transfer,
hyperconnectivity, lazy afternoons at Pete's Harbor watching the oil slick
rainbows going *rainbow rainbow rainbow*, or polishing the sheer strip

on my dad's Cal 24, the pleasure of abrasions (made by Goodyear)
on the salt effusions of the Bay, balance, a rubber dinghy,
my muttering about, my dad's muttering about, shiny in teak oil,

and my face shining off the fiberglass hull shining too your complete
annealment. Self-reflexivity, a harmonic thing "I Can See Clearly Now"
the (acid) rain has gone (Johnny Nash, newly dead) sings on the radio

listening to earth. We keep driving, but we have not listened to earth,
its jones for wreathing carbon. One theory suggests roughly 350 million years
ago some plants evolved the ability to produce lignin, a complex polymer

that made their cellulose stems much hardier, woodier. The ability
to produce lignin led to the evolution of the first trees. But bacteria and
fungi did not immediately evolve the ability to decompose lignin,

so wood didn't fully decay, became buried, sedimented, eventually
turning into coal. Then there's our anthropogenic energy transfer,
the other part of the song. I'm still struggling with the plant / tire

dichotomy, cognitive object dissonance child, or the memory of a child
that wakes ours up, and then we're home to our electric house built
in the 70s, when "natural gas" was expensive and cars were small

and bad, and crisis and energy were wedded like a very special molecule,
maybe hope, but it passed. Say you got an island, say you got a free pass,
say you went away and came back with a different circulation,

say dispersion is clarity shared among the living, the insight occurred
at Starbuck's with a collective cup gasp. Say it turned into the material
of our unsuspecting lives, spread formations that do

and do not cohere to the shape of the human. What shape the human?
though you didn't notice or care, being dumb, numb, overwhelmed
by the constant buy in of yes, or no dice, no service. Say it was

the thing in your hand blinking, a rectangular star made out of
rare earths, enduring plastics, polyethylene casings like shells
of a future crab scuttling across the floor of the silent sea.

Selah! your velvety texture lubricates me with me: it is the rapture
of our mutual lives and *I will go to the bank near the wood*
and become undisguised, I will bare our uniform hieroglyph.

Mother Ode

a, and, heir, address, what isn't one of your subjects

You, who have given me

subjects, writing sunlight, just now

through the cracked car window, falling prismatically
   on the recognized moles of my arms—they are

your arms in the warm morning air—intuited body of creases
     that covers a body, riverine channels caught
in the corner of our eyes

and the real sedge-pocketed wetlands, grassy hills,
     and brackish flows, a stand
of egrets—alone but together—scattered
         over the marsh

    All this, an image, the pictures we have
made together, walking the Kodachrome coast,
         and you too reader
just now imagining your Mother, first flash
              or glimmer
       of face
or breast, emanation of safety,
   home, smell

   from the actual marsh. It is Bair Island
in my world, a home near San Francisco, or the estuarial
     Pescadero where I place it,
     how you have
saved this real thing,
      Dear Mother, made a difference

~

What is it to make a difference?

What Progress from a thug's life, or a TV latchkey life?
I watch *60 Minutes* and hear Morley Safer down the hall...
    It is vaguely the 70s in what I am saying

This too is one of your subjects—

Free Speech, literacy, quilting, Mothers Against War,
    voter registration, happenings, chants and marches,
        I am in a gym somewhere in Oakland,
  we are there to protest Vietnam,
            we are painting placards, the primary
    colors of War—
                 foggy eucalyptus outside,
a scratchy blue sweater you made me

       ~

The earth is hot tonight with all of its angers, the human need
    a small part of the destruction, an enduring sign
        for the sentence of odes, devotions
    that kill, come out of the mouth

And it's cool, cold, freezing again in a foreign car or a small
    house on a large lake—Tahoe, Placid, Geneva, the Suisse
        affect of people we knew then
    who I dream about now,
        one of your subjects

       ~

       Genitive, direction, source of all beginning,
of what skill can we turn to avoid a hot end?

What does the poem do as a rescue to hydrogen?

What much, mulch, burn / not burn down the house or marsh?

What will the burn down be in the loss of Mother?

       ~

These aggregates grow at the bottom of the ocean
    I say this because I went sailing with my mother

She of the sea, in a driving reach, firm hand on the tiller
    coming about, or with a pen, a petition, a cup of wine
      inked by moonlight

We are birthed by care and carelessness, circumstance
    and Money, but always Mothers

  where the mouth is, where the care is

Water breaks, everyone starts out innocent
    and from a Mother, the image suffices, briefly

        a We,
      a conjoined planting

  an earth somewhere, our hands in it, something
living that will outlive the dead,
        conjunction, air, address, ah—

    say it will suffice

Precarity

Beyond vision
is a door

to see and be seen
going there

why must so much stay hidden

    the jewel
that stays shroud

that stays the crowd
faith or folly
in all

what a job
to do and see

what we need
from what's missing

•

To see and be seen
to have said and done

always the doing
to depend on

why must I do for you

    —the jewel's the jewel

for you to seem seen
in what's given

    —the jewel's the jewel

Laughing Man

When I woke this morning I was a laughing man. Not someone
waking up from a dream of laughing, nor the watching of a
man laughing suddenly awake, but a real laughing man.

I should try to explain that it was rich with others, others laughing,
a general din, but they have run away in my dream.

The dream itself was lively and tan—there was a class, a
gathering of ends of sorts of people, "fuck you, I love you!" and
"what is quantity!?" Yet this was only so interesting, and there

were places to go, parties more ribald, and people paying
for things like Lyft or tuition. But there was a visitor, and he had
come to the class in my dream and brought his girl, who could be

his wife or maybe his daughter, and she had fine sandy hair
and deep laughter lines as if she had been with him laughing
for a very long time. Thus speaks a visitor, whenever they arrive.

And he cautioned me, as she was sitting down, to brush the dust
slowly from the chair, "please don't sift dust into her eyes,
her eyes, which are fair and blue and very sensitive."

He was not laughing, he had seen a cloud darken, to lose
one's sight, one's way or sight of why fate or a teacher arrives
as a denim man who might explain why anything laughs.

What a dream! A long winter rushes up to pause the explanation,
the explanation which is not what we wish for but sunlight dreaming,
a full solar laugh, a wish-warm arrival, a burning bush.

To write release in a dream of endless fire and denim. "Yes," he said,
while he and the woman began to laugh, and to run away into the
glowing woods, a small bright astral vehicle, something sped up
with auric streamers that appeared to love life very well.

This is a picture of a laughing man leaving a party and into
the woods where there is more laughter and languid sunshine
needing no explanation and people will follow.

Why I will get up from this table and follow the sunshine
and the denim jacket of a tribe of people living outside.
Why I will make a pact with the present to not use the future

as a problem about being late. And I will leave, I have left
an old and grading life behind, and it is a sunshine to be out
in the world of laughter when there is so much pain.

The dream. It is clear there is no generation that knows
and does not know. There is no conveyor belt to happiness
and sleep though we would dream deeply to get there.

We go on in our lives not remembering the laughter
of children. Not the idea but our own bright guttural who
who has been missing for centuries. From us and to us,

my daughter rises every morning like the visitor from a dream
but she is real. She knows where to go for the sunshine
of this blue planet and the games that will make her laugh.

I am running running after her broken free

Respiration Ode

Poetry readings are real, real breathing, but the intake's
all wrong, disconnected, unpulmunarious, say you
are a performer, you must use your time wisely,
verve & salt, we are not clowns, this is a pageant
of dignity, deep breathing, true confessions
we are all clowns quite recent in human history,
some notion, perhaps wrought from the academy
that all poets should stay home and write self-expressive
poems why a blue jay could possibly land on a porch
each day anew, a new metaphor tattooed on its belly
for you, caw cause, I mean, the world intends, really,
is everyone breathing deeply as Ethel Mermen, the awkward
fumbling human figure and voice, it's a good messenger,
senses merge in the strange chasm of the throat, an O
in which I write this confusingly at my grandfather's house
in green Vermont, a lake, loons, the humidity wheezing
a kind of perfunctoriness, shortness of breath, and thank
goodness I am ranting now, for it's the clichés that kill
the dream, the bird, the bird brain, or I will read two
or three more and then I'll end, I had a boyfriend who
used to read newspapers at readings, very newsy,
facts going down like a red fire truck answering flood
but no thrall, no inhale admission—I am sad in the
abstract and angry in the real, reading this thread

alone—was his name Kenny Goldsmith? I too dislike it
and it's not difficult reading to the emotionally uncommitted,
ambrosia—another literary tote bag gleaned
from the Loom of Poetry, we don't have to balkanize
or swoon for abstraction, naming the font's frosty
glow in white space breaks your heart, so lonely
to publish any screed, you mentioned Rilke earlier,
earlier is pre when everything was new, meaning
your late comments make me laugh, and laughing's
good in the rarified comedic register of performance,
I'm in one now—Das Poetry! Das Poetry!—its unfurling
white flag of the person, let's call her Vanessa, can we
get the real person from the literal breath, who needs
a secret sharer when the O's really home, for a face
I ask Emily Dickinson, but sometimes my ass is a hat,
she didn't even read in public but she sang in living nests
to brood a birdy work, I'm all alone at the winter podium,
my voice fails me again and again, respiration,

    , inspiration,

        , it's everyone's problem

My Wife's New Desk

is a beauty, black walnut mid-century modern with a
double chevron inlay pattern of alternating English

walnut (buttery against chocolate), felled in Missouri
and shipped to Thailand to be built, to be fitted

with a teak rail that encircles the rectangle in a
glowing signal of order emblematic of Thai marquetry

or no, parquetry, the difference being the former
is the addition of a layered veneer while the latter

is the creation of a design or pattern using blocks
or strips of wood inset. My wife built it when it arrived

from Wayfair, though it would be more accurate
to say she assembled it in her new office (the son's

former bedroom) quickly converted to space that says
"stay out!" It would be more accurate to say also that

a Thai man named Asnee worked 57 hours total
smoothing the outcries of the tree into a beautiful

object that travelled back and forth in a Matson
cargo container (of Matson, Inc. HQ Honolulu and

established in 1882 as the Matson Navigation Company,
Pearl Harbor, the very moment of annexation's gather

or a vital lifeline to the economies of the greater Pacific
Rim we call today, you chose) thousands of miles with other

like same immigrant & nomadic desks delivered to
western shores. This isn't actually the first desk (or chair),

don't get me started on that (mostly Honduran) another
arriving from Wayfair or Thailand or UPS that

had a different pattern of checkerboard that was
simply too busy. This was returned via said transport

to a warehouse in Boston (Copley Place, Wayfair Inc) where
it remains unclaimed. Thai forestry practices have been evolving

since they cut down most of their own hardwoods, beginning
in 1963 (mostly teak) with the establishment of the Royal

Forest Department, which regulates the production of forest
harvest, though not the sweat shop working conditions

for Asnee and his cohort. I feel bad for them both
though good about the desk, which is uncomfortable,

which come to think of it we saw on a super tanker bejeweled
with Matson containers, white and blue layer cake floating

in the Palilolo Channel between Maui and Molokai last January.
My wife says I have a way of making stationary things move,

which is to say I kick the dog sometimes on walks and think
of the weather passing overhead over the raw and built objects

of the world in their various states of formation. I believe
the desk, which as I said is a beaut, will help the difficult

task of being and becoming that I hear my wife making /
unmaking behind the securely shut door of her escape.

Like a slow boat to China, I wish I had one too, the un-
divided space and time to see things as they really are.

Repair

> *"Together let us beat this ample field,"*
> —Alexander Pope

I set out for joy and arrive at Target, one more day
of sunshine and perplexity, the wind down Paine
    or Main or Haddock, nothing more, nothing less.
      One could sign a kind of progress, that'd be nice,
    riches, or rain, or real angels, relief in bees,
or help raking leaves, some rapper in Philly
making sunshine out of hate. But who can say
  they're two? I can't breathe you. I'm fumbling in the
    parking lot, lack of contact standing in a crowd,
      keyless entry on vague emergency, my g-g-generation
    of cloud concern, the concern psychopathology,
  local weather, or where, or whither. The tip of ice
into relative loss? Egress, shoppers! I'm shouting
    we're leaving. And where to go when the feeling's gone?

      —I loved that song. Rather to read the wise men
as a nursing scholar, study the body as a social pact,
  a gendered art, an other's functioning in fact.
Share the nuts, the slip, the slide, that's perspective
    rising from blood to brain, corrective tissue, I mean
      enlargement that has cause. Further than a tree
        and it's simply speech, nothing to stitch the phloem
      to the hutch, why it's easy to be not me,
    lining the sky with silver to make it better.

What makes something better is a common bond.
    Empathy feels a connection in the shins while
        sympathy simply pushes the shopping cart away.
Toward / away, a push me 'til I pull you
            from the sea. Is this natural selection? Sex's run?
        I write this poem because I don't know.
    Ocean's a mind of coriol signs, sedimentary gloss
            on planet rock, wince when you see what I say.

    Is it better to stand on one's own and not go out?
        Bring them kitties and newsies to my hole
before I sleep. That'd be dullness spread across,
    and spread across is sharing. Yet *bright star shines*
            the living hand, hand in the back of our back,
    at least to heft the angel out of bed, something quick
to make sweat sing, shine difference, gleam presents.

I would issue fresh fingers to ground the shot day
in all its complexity, something bound to squire loss,
    for loss is dumb and cruel and efficient, and efficiency's
  a fact of the environment, all querulous disregard for
  the obvious storm, basic thermodynamics, why each year
a new place is named. Ferguson, Minneapolis, Mobile,
          San Bernardino,
    place is a name for a violence.

My heart knows nothing, is a know nothing heart
    seeking and breeding another bleeding heart,
        little blind wealth
    of some long chain, this is empathy
I fear you will understand,
      the wr**eck**age of *empire*

  sheared on the liminal whale, end of you, I say
beginning of me. What little we seem to understand
grows farther, grows faster, offers the skin
    too quickly to fire,
        consuming
    as it wanders all that it knows.

Hey, ho, let's go...I'm really just lost in menswear
        Excuse me, the door's ajar,
And are you free today to discuss in your country's future?
        My daughter's an addict
Why at least you have a daughter!
          My marriage has died
And what a lucky fellow you are to have wed!

As I lay dying the river floods for real, a legacy floats
   over me, monstrous carp to sour fields. At least you can say you
lived! Concern, that is, there is no grandeur but ours,
     hours, these days of rancor and blown out knees.
        Believing the real emotion's in the bilge,
     why not handle the pump?
'   *Tis better to feel the hand break on wood than grow a cold.*
  Anon's coming, a fresh typhoon
engulfs an island, the bodies are stacked in palm pyres, waiting.
The atmosphere is not a perfume, why
   I rhyme to feel the sky is orange
     over Los Angeles, the sodium backflow
       of radiant gases one too.

The collective dreams hands that ache from being up.
    We're all nervous refugees in a world gun crazy.
      Call this terror or common or freedom
        Officer, can you hear me?
           It's grave and cold in my cell.
         To knock and knock and knock again,
      my head hurts you, I should stop,
    it's outrageous, we're closing,
hurry up it's time!

      It's been time a very long time. Such broken records
    of human reign wreak wreckage, litter lawns, nothing less
than harassment. Am I Bob? A glacier? Kimani Gray?
          Am I Syria, Nigeria, Gondwanaland?
I can't breathe! I fear the guards, miss the angels,
    life is jacked by a man named Deer, names
free associate, it's the same,
      epochs seen backwards from a random
         spray of blood—Aisle 4—all sad sack
       and salt pan panned.

The surface is the problem, the problem is the burn,
    everyone's skin born under the sun, sir, sere, sur, equatorial
stutter, who's not always under the sun? And who the fuck knows
    what my hands will tell? And who the fuck knows what
the heart knows? The proximate human's the sign of the visible,
    face of faces, hand in hand, easy to feel what is felt. It's the hidden
that's missing, lost envelope at the heart of our concerns, hiddenness
    itself enfolded along the sinews of a dream, shadow and light
in corners and far sutures, ghostly signs of tenderness
    working in the genome, each one different the same.

I am hungry for what I do not see and would find out by faith
    in above and below. Ariels arise! They are awake
        and shopping. I'm sputtering forward
            like Macklemore, ***problema's on the line***,
    day after day, the turn of the cart
                not material at all but vision stretched to visionary.
            Having kids, jobs, catastrophes, gear,
                my persons seek conversions,
                    and we struggle.

Remember the 18th century, and the 5th! I sense an old gyre
in the tropical breeze, tidal surge in Manilla's been traveling
a long time. It's got the daily missing in its forebody, plain sight.
One love, beasties, repair!, repair!, what joy grieves griefs joy!
So easy to twirl in the terrible search for a subject. Empathy,
and the opposite, feel it in beams that extend in all directions,
grace or grasses or platypus code, amniotic wedge,
and stem surge, it's there in the gasses
of the unmiraculous stars.

I set out for joy and reach Draco Dwarf, local satellite of our milky stuff, I can see, I look up and down with your eyes too. Wondrous calamity! Such roundness is the fruit of the spherical view, capacious jam to bind and sum, stitching our asses to the bone. Breathe, breathe, we all must breathe, earth must breathe trees, trees must breathe people, one lung, ample field, we must not break the cycle. My lover and my brother, my family and foe, to try and try to care. I care about you as you become me, my more-than-imbricate case. To be moving—I make it up out of fragments—another day admittedly a mess, but to wish or wave a felt flag is my affect to see. You hold it skyways, and I'll try.

Late Music

Feeling the lonesome sky on a long drive home, you make it so

First frost, and the Black-eyed Susans staring, apparently

"Existence precedes Essence," he said, we say

Soon you will feel a foreboding in the Winter
you have conceived

pain in the belly, a weather map of the eastern seaboard,
organ music grinding the Messiah,
a boy building an igloo covered in powder

—the wind howls ominously, see?

Rain follows fire turns to snow of ash

White, what have we done to Civilization?

There is no snowman you have not rolled from memory

Naturally, you can't always be reasonable, Humanism is
what humans do

Wash the blood from your hands

Walk to the distant farmhouse covered in crows

Spring, pack, make a pact, choose murder, lust, compassion, shame

There is no such thing as not choosing

Country Mulligan

                ...a kinder enclosure,
            bower, clover—
    the planet turns cooler, greener, bluer
  Al Gore is president and 9/11 never happened
A Moslem spring flowers into poly-Arabian nights
Scheherazadism, TwoStateism, 23andMe goes viral,
everyone's got it, Ehud Barak and Yasser Arafat
do bloodwork on TV, they're related through Mother Theresa
The Kyoto Accord begins a new epoch of collectivity,
    global council, every subject at the worship table

No jumbo anything happened anywhere ever—
The bubble never burst, and dot.com's
    greener, bluer, pinker, co-capital blooms
in the Capital, the war machine is undone
Cars get cleaner, smaller, saner, they drive themselves
  silently through the streets alone

A little boy falls into Apeland at the Cincinnati Zoo,
Harambe the Silverback, saves the boy and signals mother
to the mother, walls fall, enclosures flower over
      A jet over Ukraine flies calmly to its destination
Bashar Al Assad dies peacefully in his sleep, 2003,
  while Damascus hums under its new glass dome

Wake up C.D. Wright
Wake up Jake Adam York
Wake up Akilah Oliver
Wake up Mark Spitzer
My friends, my dogs, my next-door neighbor
  Wake up John, wake up

On a summer street in Manhattan two cops joke
with a large wheezy black man about selling copied cassettes
Officer _____ buys *Outlandas d'Amore*
We never learn the large man's name

On a quiet cul-de-sac in a non-descript golf community
north of Orlando a black teenager walks to his aunt's house
Nodding to a nodding short white man in a golf cart
He flips up his hoodie against the cool February night

A collective decrease in the actual hum
A diminution of shooting and driving and yelling
    lights growing smarter when they are unturned
  A new technology turns carbon capture into
photovoltaic glass, and coal fire burns sentient orbs
into Cleveland factories for a new millennium

In Detroit unemployment permanently drops
as the glass factory shines its new smart windows
at Delhi, Dakar, Venice and Utrecht

In East St. Louis Black & Blue have a picnic,
   play softball, give toys and socks to homeless kids
     growing stronger, softer, keener

A new species of human is discovered to have
been here all along. Lobes

in the front of the medulla oblongata light up
with photovoltaic consciousness, speaking to the
  windows who speak to the whales through
    the glittering plankton net

Sandy Hook Elementary opens a new playground
A community outreach center in San Bernardino
welcomes a new Moslem couple into the community
They have a six-year-old autistic boy named Omar

In Aurora, Colorado the Metrolux 16 goes green
and expands into a four-dimensional entertainment
center replete with hover skating, SkyFall™, and an exotic
petting zoo where the animals pet the humans
A schizophrenic youth named James enjoys the petting
and becomes a counselor for troubled teens & pets

In South Carolina, the Emanuel African Episcopal
Methodist Church celebrates 127 years of peaceful worship
and Dylan Roof gets a girlfriend, a Filipina named Viola

The new species of human begins to feel all the lonely people
in the world, and listens quietly through the morning air
Everyone's brains light up in the glass of the morning air

Difference begins a band and everyone's in it
Everyone plays their part and then some, and gets
equally paid, though not everyone plays as well, the new
humans help everyone sing with their best brains

Dolphins share an old technology of breathing
and everyone takes only as much as they need
The dolphins in their delight take the new humans
to Atlantis which turns out to be under Hawaii

My future wife, looking back in the memory glass,
pauses before the Nader bubble, shrugs, and votes for Gore

Youth become undisaffected listening to the new humans
in the band called *Difference*, their new hit: "Everyone's a Pathogen"

On an underground sea mount in the Atlantic
the other Atlanteans wake up, and open the ocean door

Meanwhile, Al Gore, after finishing up his invention
of the World Wide Web, develops the first ontologically real
inter-species think tank, and he gets in it, with the dolphins
and the new humans and the thinking glass, and they Think

    —all the dead poets wake up, and the dead friends,
        and musicians too

And all the dead painters wake up

    and the dancers too   and the wounded

    and all the lonely people undone & bored by slight
        and painful things
           to think—

a kinder enclosure, a bower
                            InterClover

              a planet turned cooler
              turned greener & bluer

A Field Mentality

New content, new time
Mei Mei Berssenbrugge says
on our Afterlives

*duration continues what has
passed with now*

What has passed with now?

In a scalar sky *two birds
perch in a constellation tree,
subtle, entangled*

a you that is following me,
the weight of your gaze
falling outside time

What is field is felt, a sprig
of bad weather or an algae
bloom driven by wildfire

O

You are the voice
inside the engine
Earth so

tell us
how to cure
our avarice

The Weight

Arrested by light, the weight.
Cloud crowns billowed
into a porcelain chief's head.
The chief's head loomed
over a real shadow island.

We were here, we were
there, madeshattered, a time
ly paradise, caring and carrying
the weight of the world
is love, he sd, obsessed

with angels and burdens, a vision
of skin. I repeat it, to carry,
to instruct the body through dreams
and dissatisfactions,
solitude and its excess
es, no rest without love.

Light draws the chief's head
down into yours, the weight.
The warm eye opens, we move
to the center, enburdened
and saved by the weight.

Bouquet

i

fleur   a word taken from the road
the road answering   flipside's
    inevitable black line
fragile travel   in winter's vest   trying
trying to get home

or 43 miles to Keane   a comfort in
"I'm gonna love you 'til daybreak"
blue bells or daylilies or the lilies
on the sheets   love

a picture taken from the road
the road a line of corn   memories
window's toes   meaning my heart
in pictures   delirious vacation of flowers

this vast circuit of exhalations
shockingly different every day
    a different meaning   meaning
fragile   the snowflakes unevenly

driving white line of attention
season sung   a vast circuit
a flower taken from the road

ii

tassel-view turning   Bloom day
June tree turning day on

if it is day that sings   sings like a voice
full of sunshine   blacktop   dandelion
   and something catches

advancement of rays   all hooks
               it will be sun
   in your eyes over the roaring prairie

dinosaurs to the left of you   golden buffalo
to the right   yaw   the be more drawn
            of telluric objects
in the dumpwork of space

paintbrush   red light   cosmic deposit
the local jug giving   giving way   turning
brown scour of wind   the direction of wind

if you watch the sun   golden
do not watch the sun   turning away
what I've told you

gambling's good   a million lbs
days and the sun and we still
watch   gambling on space

•

there is blossom in looking

iii

a red I can trust
and the need for red

a blood red citizen
blood   for the citizen
or a hydrant gushing away

you see it there   burst flower
hill and dale   street scuffle
any place or ferrous future

what land's not a message
measure   obliged to be born
we begin again

        courage   corsage   carnation—

red flame's burgeon   sunseting wind
       beams directly flying
  our enormous speed

not red at all but bruise
at rest   or a metal object
rusting away

we trust color
to be the measure of things

  flags   guns   faces   skins
the distance growing   growing near

    I color trust in a private room

the sun shines all the colors all the time

iv

run yellow dream   how the flower was
    the imaginer   portal
by pistil a built up bloom

condensery of light and fragrance
there was so much fragrance
the bright side life of

cause   the pond   its animal
    treading spore

smells everyday   reasons
    heliotropics
beds   and paths

this dream imaginer tends
portal to fall through
and plant   and paw

•

until the animal is seen

under our bright side life

all the planets go dark

v

    the geography of darkness   aloud
    who doesn't love the country
        country   a song
    taken from the road

    beyond the hedge a blight
    a dark air rising   coal   caw
    country   continent

        containment

                Bouquet—

    the little people peopling the big
    human machinery what passes
    for gestures   home

    landfill   landfill   <small>landfill</small>
    a wait in the shade under a tulip tree
    forgive us   our marvels

    stacks of shells   sells
    for a time   a roadside attraction
    improvements   new ducks
    gold derricks minting streams

    the markings of progress
    by hook and drive

    anthem   anodyne   aloud

    the little hands
    the little hands stitch new flowers...

Notes

the atmosphere is not a perfume it is odorless has been a curiously durational project. The book was started in the double shadow of 9/11 and the George W. Bush presidency. The first poems written—"Snow Gobe," "No Ode" and "Postlude"—date their origins back to 2003 or 4. A kind of witness, a kind of love, I hoped to embody some cellular resistance through a series of occasional odes. Needless to say the occasions and revisions just kept coming. More specifics:

• "Precarity" ["*The sad marvels...*"] quotes from George Oppen's "Of Being Numerous."

• "No Ode" riffs on and magnetizes off: Psalm 73:25, The Talking Heads, Goethe, Charles Olson, Wallace Stevens, Gerald Stern, Susan B. Anthony, Pseudo-Dionysius and, most notably, Allen Ginsberg, whose poem "Wales Visitation" is quoted extensively in Part II.

• "General Syntax" and "Major Lure" are constructed largely from speeches made by General Douglas MacArthur, most notably his "Farewell Address to Congress," April 19, 1951.

• "Gun Ode" riffs on, and is in conversation with Allen Ginsberg's famous ode "America."

• "Song" is a titration of Allen Ginsberg's poem "Song"; "The Weight" is a translocation / rehabilitation of the same Ginsberg poem.

• "Wall Ode" plays on Shakespeare's Sonnet XII, the concluding line, "Save breed, to brave him when he takes thee hence."

• "Difference Essay" makes reference to, and quotes variously, numerous sources. See footnotes for specifics.

• "Appears / Disappears" and "Hive's Lament," both original poems, were written in an exchange with the English poet Lawrence Upton, 1949-2020, as a commission for *likestarlings*.

• "the atmosphere is not a perfume it is odorless" opens and closes with lines from Walt Whitman's "Song of Myself," Sec. 2; brief shimmers go to Elizabeth Bishop's "The Fish," as well Queen (and Freddy Mercury). The poem also google mines metadata on fossil fuels from various sources.

- "Repair" was written out of a collision of texts: Robert Duncan's *HD Book*, Alexander Pope's "Essay on Man," Claudia Rankine's *Citizen*, and Ryan Lewis & Macklemore's *The Heist*, in particular the song "Same Love."

- "My Wife's New Desk" plays off of Wallace Stevens' "The Man with the Blue Guitar."

- "Late Music" is in conversation with Jean Paul-Sartre's essay "Existentialism as Humanism."

- "A Field Mentality" engages Mei Mei Berssenbrugge's poem "Scalar," from *A Treatise on Stars*.

- the last line of "Bouquet" is from Louis Zukofsky's book *80 Flowers*.

Acknowledgments

A heartfelt thanks to the following journals, editors and publishers who believed in these poems, and published them, sometimes in different forms. A deep well of appreciation to readers, friends and mentors who helped this long song along: Peter Balakian, Julie Carr, Carol Ciavonne, Ben Evans, Gillian Conoley, Timothy Donnelly, Michael Dumanis, Camille Dungy, John Gallaher, Stephanie G'Schwind, Joe Harrington, Brenda Hillman, Robert Hass, Hoag Holmgren, Marius Lehene, Khaled Mattawa, Joshua McKinney, Jeffrey Pethybridge, Louann Reid, Luke Rolfes, Todd Simmons, Sara Tekula, Dan Beachy-Quick and Sasha Steensen. Thank you to Editors Extraordinaire Jon Thompson and David Blakesley for believing in the project. Finally, to my family, and their patiences: outer circle of Coopermans and Kaupangs, and inner circle of Elias, Maya, and my love, Aby Kaupang, "I would meet you anywhere western sun meets the air."

•

"Of Poses," "Wall Ode," "My Wife's New Desk," *Laurel Review*
"Precarity," [The sad marvels...], *SPACECRAFTPROJECT*
"Precarity," [to see and be seen / by others...], *SPACECRAFTPROJECT*
"Precarity," [beyond vision / is a door...] *SPACECRAFTPROJECT*
"Precarity," [the be in "A"...] *SPACECRAFTPROJECT*
"Precarity," [to see and be seen / by a specialist...],
    MARY: A Journal of New Writing
"Snow Globe," "No Ode," "Postlude," *Fogged Clarity*
"General Syntax," "Major Lure," *Kenyon Review Online*
"Gun Ode," "Late Music," *Michigan Quarterly Review*
"Difference Essay," *Seattle Review*
"Appears / Disappears," "Hive's Lament," *Likestarlings*
"the atmosphere is not a perfume it is odorless," "A Field Mentality," *Prelude*
"Repair," *Bennington Review*
"Mother Ode," "Laughing Man," "Respiration Ode," *Posit*
"Country Mulligan," *Mudlark*
"Standing Figures," *VOLT*
"Bouquet," *The Literary Review*

About the Author

Poet, critic, editor, educator and collaborator, Matthew Cooperman's work plies the interdisciplinary boundaries of poetry, ecopoetics, ethnography and visual arts. He is the author of, most recently, *Wonder About The*, winner of the Halcyon Prize (Middle Creek Publishing, 2023), as well as *NOS* (*disorder, not otherwise specified*), with Aby Kaupang, (Futurepoem, 2018), *Spool*, winner of the New Measure Prize (Free Verse Editions/Parlor Press, 2016), the text + image collaboration *Imago for the Fallen World*, with Marius Lehene (Jaded Ibis Press, 2013), *Still: of the Earth as the Ark which Does Not Move* (Counterpath Press, 2011) and other books. Recent poems and criticism have appeared in such places as *Prelude, Lana Turner, Heavy Feather Review,* and *The Laurel Review*. A Professor of English at Colorado State University, he is also co-poetry editor for *Colorado Review*. He lives in Fort Collins with his wife, the poet Aby Kaupang, and their two children. http://matthew-cooperman.org

Photograph of the author by Matthew Cooperman. Used by permission.

Free Verse Editions

Edited by Jon Thompson

13 ways of happily by Emily Carr
& in Open, Marvel by Felicia Zamora
& there's you still thrill hour of the world to love by Aby Kaupang
Alias by Eric Pankey
the atmosphere is not a perfume it is odorless by Matthew Cooperman
At Your Feet (A Teus Pés) by Ana Cristina César, edited by Katrina Dodson,
    trans. by Brenda Hillman and Helen Hillman
Bari's Love Song by Kang Eun-Gyo, translated by Chung Eun-Gwi
Between the Twilight and the Sky by Jennie Neighbors
Blood Orbits by Ger Killeen
The Bodies by Christopher Sindt
The Book of Isaac by Aidan Semmens
The Calling by Bruce Bond
Canticle of the Night Path by Jennifer Atkinson
Child in the Road by Cindy Savett
Civil Twilight by Giles Goodland
Condominium of the Flesh by Valerio Magrelli, trans. by Clarissa Botsford
Contrapuntal by Christopher Kondrich
Country Album by James Capozzi
Cry Baby Mystic by Daniel Tiffany
The Curiosities by Brittany Perham
Current by Lisa Fishman
Day In, Day Out by Simon Smith
Dear Reader by Bruce Bond
Dismantling the Angel by Eric Pankey
Divination Machine by F. Daniel Rzicznek
Elsewhere, That Small by Monica Berlin
Empire by Tracy Zeman
Erros by Morgan Lucas Schuldt
Extinction of the Holy City by Bronisław Maj, trans. by Daniel Bourne
Fifteen Seconds without Sorrow by Shim Bo-Seon, trans. by Chung Eun-Gwi
    and Brother Anthony of Taizé
The Forever Notes by Ethel Rackin
The Flying House by Dawn-Michelle Baude
General Release from the Beginning of the World by Donna Spruijt-Metz
Ghost Letters by Baba Badji
Go On by Ethel Rackin
Here City by Rick Snyder
An Image Not a Book by Kylan Rice
Instances: Selected Poems by Jeongrye Choi, trans. by Brenda Hillman, Wayne de
    Fremery, & Jeongrye Choi

Invitatory by Molly Spencer
Last Morning by Simon Smith
The Magnetic Brackets by Jesús Losada, trans. by M. Smith & L. Ingelmo
Man Praying by Donald Platt
A Map of Faring by Peter Riley
The Miraculous Courageous by Josh Booton
Mirrorforms by Peter Kline
A Myth of Ariadne by Martha Ronk
No Shape Bends the River So Long by Monica Berlin & Beth Marzoni
North | Rock | Edge by Susan Tichy
Not into the Blossoms and Not into the Air by Elizabeth Jacobson
Overyellow, by Nicolas Pesquès, translated by Cole Swensen
Parallel Resting Places by Laura Wetherington
pH of Au by Vanessa Couto Johnson
Physis by Nicolas Pesquès, translated by Cole Swensen
Pilgrimage Suites by Derek Gromadzki
Pilgrimly by Siobhán Scarry
Poems from above the Hill & Selected Work by Ashur Etwebi, trans. by Brenda Hillman & Diallah Haidar
The Prison Poems by Miguel Hernández, trans. by Michael Smith
Puppet Wardrobe by Daniel Tiffany
Quarry by Carolyn Guinzio
remanence by Boyer Rickel
Republic of Song by Kelvin Corcoran
Rumor by Elizabeth Robinson
Settlers by F. Daniel Rzicznek
A Short History of Anger by Joy Manesiotis
Signs Following by Ger Killeen
Small Sillion by Joshua McKinney
Split the Crow by Sarah Sousa
Spine by Carolyn Guinzio
Spool by Matthew Cooperman
Strange Antlers by Richard Jarrette
A Suit of Paper Feathers by Nate Duke
Summoned by Guillevic, trans. by Monique Chefdor & Stella Harvey
Sunshine Wound by L. S. Klatt
System and Population by Christopher Sindt
These Beautiful Limits by Thomas Lisk
They Who Saw the Deep by Geraldine Monk
The Thinking Eye by Jennifer Atkinson
This History That Just Happened by Hannah Craig
An Unchanging Blue: Selected Poems 1962–1975 by Rolf Dieter Brinkmann, trans. by Mark Terrill
Under the Quick by Molly Bendall
Verge by Morgan Lucas Schuldt

The Visible Woman by Allison Funk
The Wash by Adam Clay
Well by Sasha Steensen
We'll See by Georges Godeau, trans. by Kathleen McGookey
What Stillness Illuminated by Yermiyahu Ahron Taub
Winter Journey [Viaggio d'inverno] by Attilio Bertolucci, trans. by
 Nicholas Benson
Wonder Rooms by Allison Funk

www.ingramcontent.com/pod-product-compliance
Lightning Source LLC
Chambersburg PA
CBHW041141170426
43200CB00022B/2991